Husbands, Pray With Your Wives

John Henry

This edition first published in paperback by
Michael Terence Publishing in 2024
www.mtp.agency

Copyright © 2024 John Henry

John Henry has asserted the right to be identified as
the author of this work in accordance with the
Copyright, Designs and Patents Act 1988

ISBN 9781800948860

No part of this publication may be reproduced, stored
in a retrieval system, or transmitted, in any form or
by any means, electronic, mechanical, photocopying,
recording or otherwise, without the prior
permission of the publisher

Cover design
Michael Terence Publishing
www.mtp.agency

Michael Terence
Publishing

Introduction

Husband, your wife is God's most precious earthly gift to you.

How brilliant that He has blessed you with a wonderful partner for life. It is fitting then, that you made those promises to love her, cherish her and to be faithful to her – caring for her, for better, for worse; for richer, for poorer; in sickness and in health; till death parts you.

Praying with your wife, day by day, is part of caring for her.

Our Father In Heaven

Chapter One

WHY PRAY?

1: God wants you to

He knows everything about both of you and praying together is a way of acknowledging that you want the Lord to be at the centre of your relationship.

You prayed about being married, didn't you?

Now you have a wife, God wants you to pray together to show your joint dependence on him.

Holy Is Your Name

2: Praying is a privilege

Talking with God in prayer is a tender, yet powerful expression of faith.

As husband and wife, sharing this privilege will become a joy and a source of strength in your marriage.

Prayer is a privilege because Jesus encourages us to pray about anything at any time.

He is King of kings and Lord of lords and yet his ear is always open to us.

Your Kingdom Come

3: Christians are in a spiritual battle

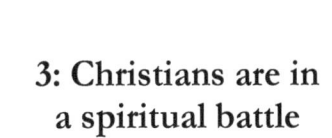

There are constant attacks on our values and beliefs. The Scriptures encourage us to 'pray at all times' (Ephesians, chapter 6, verse 18). Praying with your wife will help you both to stand firm and grow in your faith. You are a team and praying together will strengthen the unity between you.
A united team will be a victorious team.

Your Will Be Done

4: A closer relationship with God and with each other

Prayer is an intimate conversation with our Creator. Praying together helps to draw you closer to God and to each other.

The time spent together in prayer becomes special. It is sacred and precious.

Thanking the Lord together for the blessings of the day, or bringing needs to him, encourages greater closeness and understanding.

On Earth

5: Communication and openness

For your marriage to be the best that it can be there has to be good communication and openness between you and your wife.

Having a regular time to pray together encourages this. Talking about what has happened through the day before you pray, involves being together and listening to each other.

This helps your prayers to be relevant and specific.

As It Is In Heaven

6: Responsibility and covering

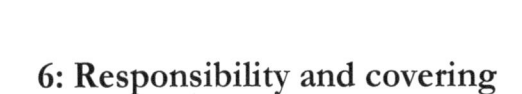

As a husband you have a responsibility from God to be concerned for your wife's welfare.

This includes all aspects of her life, including her spiritual well-being. She needs you to be praying for her and she needs you to be praying with her.

As you pray with her she will feel strengthened and encouraged. This is part of the spiritual covering she should expect from you.

Give Us This Day

7: Cherishing and caring

In giving you a wife God has greatly blessed you. He has brought you together for all sorts of reasons and one of them is that you may cherish her.

The word 'cherish' means 'to tend lovingly'. Praying with your wife is a demonstration of cherishing her.

Bringing any concerns or problems she has to the Lord as you pray together is an obvious way of showing how much you care for her.

Our Daily Bread

8: Faith, hope and love

We are told in 1 Corinthians, chapter 13, verse 13, that faith, hope and love always remain. They are constant and eternal and so must be hugely important and worth prioritising.

When you pray with your wife that is what you are doing. Together you are exercising faith as you bring your praise, thanks and requests to him.

Hope will increase as you look to God to provide for all your needs and to guide you in your marriage. Love will grow because this is a shared, intimate activity and will result in increasing closeness to Jesus and to each other.

And Forgive Us Our Sins

Chapter Two

WHY HUSBANDS MAY NOT PRAY WITH THEIR WIVES

Introduction

With all that has been suggested in Chapter One, it would seem obvious that husbands should pray with their wives on a regular basis.

Unfortunately, many husbands choose not to. It is not because they do not love God or because they do not love their wives. There are several possible reasons…

1: Too busy or preoccupied

This husband may believe that praying with his wife is important, if there is time, but not as important as other priorities.

He is involved with many legitimate pursuits and praying together just cannot be fitted in. He is reluctant to change his schedule as he is convinced that he has made the right choices.

As We Forgive Those

2: Too shy or embarrassed

Taking the initiative to suggest praying with your wife takes courage and spiritual strength.

The shy or embarrassed husband may think that he is not spiritual enough to pray with his wife or might believe that he doesn't have the words to say or the faith to pray with a believing heart.

He possibly thinks that if his wife wanted to pray with him she would suggest it, but secretly he hopes that she won't.

Who Sin Against Us

3: Too tired or lazy

Prayer takes energy. Anyone talking with God needs to be alert and focussed and, if praying with someone else, attentive to what they are saying.

The husband who tells himself, or his wife, that he is too tired to pray with her is really saying he can't be bothered.

Spiritual laziness is the root of this excuse.

And Lead Us Not Into Temptation

4: Too worldly or carnal

The husband who has allowed the things of this world to take God's place in his life will not be wanting to pray with his wife.

He will have his mind on what others think of him rather than what God thinks. He is listening to the voices of people rather than seeking God's truth. Their approval is more important than that of the Lord.

He is being led by worldly ideas instead of allowing the Holy Spirit to lead him.

But Deliver Us From Evil

5: Too selfish and self-centred

Praying with your wife involves time and consideration.

The selfish husband will put his own interests first and be blind to the needs of his wife. He may provide for all of her physical requirements but give little thought to her spiritual well-being.

This husband is not necessarily too busy to pray with his wife but is so self absorbed that it doesn't occur to him that this could be very helpful to both of them, and consequently to their marriage.

For Yours Is The Kingdom

6: Too ashamed or guilty

The husband who has unconfessed sin in his life will not be wanting to pray with his wife.

He will not feel able to sincerely pray with her when he knows he is not right with God.

Until he seeks forgiveness he will be very reluctant to pray.

The Power

7: Too worried or anxious

Sometimes life can be very difficult.

The husband who does not take his worries and anxieties to Jesus will be too burdened to pray with his wife.

Instead of receiving God's peace and strength there will be increasing tension and stress.

And The Glory

8: Too proud or self-assured

This husband believes that his spiritual life, and that of his wife, should be developed separately.

Praying with his wife is almost a sign of weakness. It is up to him to sort things out with God and for his wife to fit in with whatever is decided.

He does not believe that he and his wife are equal members of a very special team that God has joined together for the purpose of serving Jesus.

For Ever And Ever

Conclusion

You want to be a good husband and to make your wife happy. Great! That is exactly what God wants. He asks you to, 'Love your wife as Christ loved the Church and gave himself up for her' (Ephesians, chapter 6, verse 23).

Such love can only come from God. He is the source of all love and Jesus set the pattern for us to follow. He prayed with his disciples and taught them how to pray.

Holding your wife's hand and quietly saying the 'Lord's Prayer' ('Our Father') is a wonderful way to begin praying together. As you step out in faith, God will guide you…

Create the time and space that you are both comfortable with, ask the Lord to bless and lead you, and the Holy Spirit will bring to mind the things he wants you both to pray about.

Feel free for either one of you to pray and don't be anxious about short silences. Jesus can speak to you and prompt you in those times.

Reading a portion of Scripture together before praying may help to focus your mind on the Lord.

Just make a start and trust God to richly bless you both.

Amen